# BLUFF [illegible]

# ES[illegible]



PHIL KIMBY

RAVETTE BOOKS

Published by Ravette Books Limited
3 Glenside Estate, Star Road
Partridge Green, Horsham,
West Sussex RH13 8RA
(0403) 710392



Cover design – Jim Wire
Typesetting – System Graphics Ltd.
Printing & Binding – Cox & Wyman Ltd.
Production – Oval Projects Ltd.

The Bluffer's Guides are based on
an original idea by Peter Wolfe.

# CONTENTS

# INTRODUCTION

## What is Espionage?

Bluffers must know what espionage really is.

Ignore the dictionary definition. Forget what the experts claim espionage to be. Nowadays everyone is an expert, since it is becoming increasingly hard to find someone who hasn't been asked to work for the: KGB, CIA, GRU, SIS, MI5, FBI, Special Branch or the Anti-Blood Sports League, all of which involve espionage to some degree or another. And often dressing up in silly disguises.

Bluffers can indeed argue that since espionage is the growth industry of the 20th century, and since espionage is labour intensive, we probably all work for one or another of the agencies concerned, whether we know it or not. Bluffers must also know that there are as many working definitions of espionage as there are secret police in Saudi Arabia. But the only one that you need to worry about is that which, if applied to *your* own activites, could lead to:

a) your phone being tapped
b) interrogations by men who may lack a certain sympathy for your activities
c) a lucrative publishing contract
d) an early retirement somewhere it's difficult to spend any of the money from your lucrative publishing contract.

Espionage, then, can be defined as the 'unauthorised attempt by a person or persons to obtain or transmit information of any sort and so threaten the security of the State. Or help anyone else to do the same. Or even suspect that someone else is doing the same, and not say anything about it'. What you have to remember is that the State decides who is or who is not authorised, and what information will in fact threaten its security, so anything can be classified as espionage. Even if it is espionage of a rather trivial type and not to be taken too seriously.

Bluffers must also note that the act does not need to be successful to be classed as espionage: just trying is enough.

Whatever espionage may be, one thing is sure: there's an awful lot of it about, and not all of it is wasted. In fact, the bluffer can legitimately point out that the money devoted to espionage worldwide (between twenty four and thirty billion pounds sterling a year) must achieve something, and indeed it does. For example, espionage:

1. Helps relax political tensions by enabling one side to know (or think it knows) what the other side is doing. Or about to do. Or would have done if the other side hadn't found out.
2. Directly employs well over a million people; and indirectly (writers, movie technicians, journalists, etc.) probably over a million more.
3. Pleases armchair fantasists everywhere.

Overall, bluffers must realise that there are few, if any, great disasters or successes in the world of espionage, only a series of skirmishes . . . with temporary victory going to the side with the best press and public relations.

# THE PLAYERS

In order to bluff the amateur and be taken part seriously by the professional, the bluffer should know something about the world's intelligence agencies. Not a lot, because (as someone involved) you wouldn't want to divulge too much anyway. But it will help you establish whether someone else is bluffing, as well as occasionally allowing you to score points off a know-it-all at a dinner party.

It is probably easier if you learn to think of these agencies in terms of sporting leagues – remembering, of course, that Imperial Britain versus Imperial Russia on the North West Frontier used to be known as the 'Great Game'. At least by the British. The Russians took it rather more seriously, which explains why they're still playing in Afghanistan. The British knew the match was over long ago, but the Russians are still waiting for the second half.

Bluffers should note that within specific 'divisions' of the world espionage league, it is impossible to show an overall champion, except perhaps Israel which remains the top intelligence and security team. Against that, it tends to play against weaker teams more often (i.e. the Arabs), although bluffers should also know that the KGB maintains an entire department targeted specifically against Israel, while the US is lumped together with Canada. (This rather annoys the Canadians, who resent being thought of as another American state. Informed sources suggest that the KGB have agreed to give Canada its own department in exchange for extra cod and salmon quotas for the Soviet fishing fleet.)

Both China and Japan find it a little difficult to spy on Warsaw Pact countries since they tend to stand out in a crowd. As a consequence, they have been forced to spend most of their time spying on:

a) each other
b) Korea
c) each other spying on Korea.

In recognition of their own paranoia, the Koreans call their own agency the CIA. The official reason is that the letters KIA, as originally planned, and standing for Korean Intelligence Agency, also stand for Killed in Action.

All emerging nations (never say emerging from what) now see the possession of espionage and counter espionage agencies as being proof positive that they should be allowed the key to the executive washroom at the United Nations.

## Division One

| Country | Agency and Function | Professional Rating |
|---|---|---|
| *Us:* | | |
| USA | CIA – espionage | B |
| | FBI – counter espionage and major federal crimes | B- |
| | NSA – electronic surveillance | B |
| | DIA – military intelligence, often referred to as G2 | B- |
| | BIR – State Department's own private CIA and a very private agency indeed | ? |
| Britain | SIS – espionage | A |
| | MI5 – counter espionage and counter terrorism | B+ |
| | GCHQ – electronic surveillance | A- |
| | DIS – military intelligence | B+ |

| | | |
|---|---|---|
| France | DGSE – espionage | B- |
| | DST – counter espionage and counter terrorism | B+ |
| | Deuxième Bureau – military intelligence | B+ |
| West Germany | BND – espionage | B- |
| | BfV – counter espionage and counter terrorism | A |
| | MAD – military intelligence | B+ |
| *Sometimes Us:* | | |
| Israel | Mossad – espionage | A+ |
| | Shin Beth – counter espionage | A+ |
| | Aman – military intelligence, and electronic surveillance | A |
| *Them:* | | |
| Soviet Union | KGB – you name it, they do it | B |
| | GRU – military intelligence | B+ |

Of our side's Division One players, the Israelis are accepted as being the best, if the most ruthless; the Americans are bigger than anyone else but suffer from information overload and too much bureaucracy; the British are good on analysis, but are prone to periodic leaks; the French are severe, but often a little confused; and the West Germans suffer from too much political control and being everyone's favourite venue.

On the other side, the two major players are the Soviet's KGB and the GRU. Unfortunately they are major players throughout the world and dominate all games.

The KGB is not, as is popularly supposed, the direct

descendant of Cheka, the Tsar's Secret Police, or the Revolution's NKVD. It is an amalgamation of several different agencies, including one set up by Lenin for the sole purpose of stealing industrial and commercial secrets from the West. True, the KGB also includes elements of Cheka's descendants, but it is concerned with far more than merely liquidating the enemies of the State (i.e. the OGPU and James Bond's Smersh – which did actually once exist). The KGB also supplies all the border guards and maintains relations (control) with all other Warsaw Pact intelligence services.

The GRU is primarily concerned with military espionage and security, and operates abroad wherever the Soviet Union considers it to be of possible military strategic importance. That is, everywhere. The GRU may or may not be subordinate to the KGB: it all depends on who has (temporarily) won the continuing Soviet power fight between the Party, the KGB and the Armed Forces.

Bluffers should know that both the KGB and GRU maintain their own press agencies – *Tass* for the KGB (although now perhaps threatened by a Foreign Ministry and/or Party takeover), and *Novosti* for the GRU.

The Soviet Union frequently calls upon its substitutes, other Warsaw Pact intelligence agencies, of which the most important are:

1. the East German SSD (Ministry for Security and Intelligence)
2. the Czechoslovakian STB (State Secret Security).

The SSD is used by Moscow primarily to discover:

– what is happening in West Germany
– what the Cubans are up to.

The STB is often used by the Soviets to recruit foreign sources, probably because the Czechs are more European and find it easier to mix and move in the West.

Bluffers should also be aware that all Warsaw Pact agencies are:

a) deemed to be reserves of the KGB or GRU
b) often bothered about where their loyalties lie, their own country or Russia, with the exception of the Poles, who are only loyal to Russia on the third Tuesday of each month and to the Vatican secret service on alternate Sundays.

**Divisions Two and Three**

Bluffers must know that the main difference between Division One on the one hand, Divisions Two and Three on the other, is that the latter play fewer away games, i.e. do not operate quite as much internationally. While they do play host to visiting agencies from the First Division, they have little opportunity to develop certain necessary skills, like forging foreign passports.

China and South Africa are showing signs of soon being able to move up into the big time, meanwhile Australia may well be forced into Division One simply because the Pacific Rim is being widely tipped as the site of the next Espionage cup. If this happens, bluffers may expect certain transfers between Australia and China, since both are equally nervous about the USA and Japan. Canadian espionage is mainly devoted to stopping the USA and USSR playing their away games in neutral territory, i.e. Canada.

You should be aware that though Syria belongs in Division Three, its Air Force Intelligence belongs firmly in Division Two, possibly One. But do not speculate too loudly about Syrian Air Force Intelligence. The Syrians won't like it, nor will the Israelis. You can, however, claim that Iraqi counter espionage appears to be one of the few with a sense of humour, as witness the Christmas card sent to a freelance Western agent after he had spent three months in solitary, then been deported on suspicion (accurate) of planning an assassination. The message on the card read: 'Looking forward to seeing you next year.'

**Division Two**

| Country | Feels threatened by | Rating |
|---|---|---|
| *Us:* | | |
| Canada | USSR; USA | B |
| Australia | Their enormous coastline | B+ |
| Switzerland | Irresponsible fiduciary policies | B |
| Italy | Stable government | B |
| Holland | Whatever interferes with trade | B |
| Belgium | Loss of African influence | B- |
| Sweden & Norway | Not being taken seriously by the rest of the world | B- |
| *Them:* | | |
| China | USSR; Japan; USA | B |
| South Africa | Everyone, except Israel | B |

**Division Three**

| | | |
|---|---|---|
| *Us:* | | |
| New Zealand | Being noticed by any of the great powers | B- |
| *Not one of Us nor one of Them:* | | |
| South America | All South America | B- |
| *Them:* | | |
| Libya | Being ignored | B- |
| Syria* | USA and Iraq | B- |
| Iraq* | USA and Syria | B- |

*While Syria and Iraq may, at some time, feel threatened by Israel, they would never admit to it, largely because neither country recognises Israel, and how can one be threatened by something that doesn't exist?

### Division Four

This includes the rest of the world. Bluffers should note that certain countries are in the Fourth Division largely because they stubbornly refuse to play either home or away matches against other teams. It is not necessary to know what the agencies are called. It might even be considered a bit flash to know, for example, the name of Indonesia's overseas intelligence agency. What is worse, it could bring you to the attention of a Malaysian intelligence agency who might try to recruit you with promises of Kuala Lumpur by moonlight plus free batik for the rest of your life.

### Amateur Leagues

As in other sports, the standard of amateur espionage agencies is often higher than that of the professionals. Mostly, amateur agencies are those that belong to no recognised country, such as:

- the Mafia, which maintains an extremely competent espionage and counter espionage system with a little help from its friends
- the Vatican, which while theoretically a country, is really little more than a large cathedral offset by a radio station, museum and bank, but nonetheless operates one of the largest intelligence services in the world.

Japan also has to be included in this league, for although it is definitely a country, its large private corporations are mainly used for intelligence gathering overseas. Bluffers should know that there is considerable pressure from the United States for Japan's amateur status to be revoked. This is echoed by the USSR, who would dearly love to play an away game or two in Tokyo.

### Alliances

In the West, the basic alliances are between:

- the British and the Americans (SIS/CIA)
- the Americans and the Israelis (CIA/Mossad)
- the British and the West Germans (SIS,DIA/BfV)
- the West Germans and the Israelis (BND,BfV/ Mossad, Shin Beth)
- the French and the French.

The French, unfortunately, are still suffering from the rumour that its DGSE agency effectively went freelance some years ago (and certainly there were times when it showed little sign of working for the French government or for France). New brooms have swept clean, so clean that there appear to be few, if any, agents left in the DGSE, and it may be some time before it begins to function again.

Overall, there is a general awkwardness felt by other agencies in dealing with the FBI, since so many FBI personnel are:

- accountants
- lawyers
- still reporting to J. Edgar Hoover.

However, the general principle is that anyone will deal with anyone if there's good reason. And that includes deals between, say, SIS and the KGB if it means getting rid of a particularly nasty terrorist group that is bothering both.

# THE ESPIONAGE GAME

At first sight, the unwary will assume that there are only two occupations in espionage:

1. Spies – i.e. the ones who do the spying and their back up personnel
2. Counter spies – i.e. the ones who try to stop them doing it.

But the bluffer should know that this is not quite correct, for in order to do their job properly, counter spies must know what the other side's spies are planning, which means doing a little quiet spying themselves.

In fact, espionage is concerned with two main activities:

1. Intelligence (trying to find out as much as possible)
2. Security (trying to stop anyone finding out anything at all).

There is a subdivision to each category:

1.a. Intelligence security (trying to stop anyone finding out what you're trying to find out)

2.a. Security intelligence (trying to find out what someone else is trying to find out about you).

Traditionally, the glamour jobs have always been in Intelligence and Security Intelligence, if only because they allow for a cetain amount of foreign travel, or at least a share in the duty-frees of those who do. Bluffers should know, however, that all four categories are invariably called something quite different, often by people within the same agency. This adds to the normal turmoil, since people can become a little confused as to what they're supposed to be doing: Intelligence? Security? Intelligence Security Intelligence? It takes a complex mind to figure out what you're supposed to be doing, let alone start doing it.

It is important to learn something about 'the intelligence process' because this is basic to espionage. Nowadays it is customary to talk of the 'intelligence jig-saw', i.e. the act of piecing together all the separate bits of information gained by espionage, and other means, to build up the 'big picture'. This process and these phrases are invaluable, since they:

a. effectively disguise the fact that you've spent a lot of time and money gaining useless information ("But when we begin to see the big picture . . .")
b. justify the employment of thousands of analysts
c. help increase budgets (it is a well known fact that government departments love pouring money into projects which will never be completed, and thus can never be judged a failure.)

Obviously, information is the key to building up the intelligence jig-saw. But you should appreciate that, just as the jig-saw is never completed, both the individual pieces and the big picture change shape all the time. Often it becomes apparent that the picture you thought you were trying to build up never really existed.

## How It Works

Information (data) is collected by a variety of means, some overt (openly), some covert (secretly). This is a fine distinction, for even if an espionage organisation (agency) has gained information quite legally, no-one should know they have it, therefore it must be secret. However, once the opposition know that you're interested in information that's freely available, they'll make it secret themselves. So you might as well treat it as such from the beginning, and save them the trouble.

All this means that information can be gained from:

- blackmail
- theft
- photography
- listening to gossip
- reading
- thinking up good ideas in the bath.

Once collected, many minions will have to spend days, weeks, months doing the following:

**collating** the data – arranging it in some sort of recognisable, even logical, order or opening up nice, shiny new files, or computer files, both of which will immediately become secret.

**interpreting** the data – figuring out what it means, and where it fits in to the big picture.

**disseminating** the data – getting it to the people who *need to know* it.

**re-tasking** – getting back to the original data collectors in the light of the latest interpretation (e.g. finding out if the new Soviet submarine really has been designed to look and sound like a whale).

Bluffers will have noticed the italicised phrase 'need to know', which means that you only get to know the information you need to know in order to do your job. And since someone else decides what you need to know, they'll invariably err on the side of caution. As a result:

- many people in espionage spend a good deal of time working in the dark, literally and metaphorically
- senior personnel spend far too much time figuring out what their underlings *do* need to know
- many operations are bungled because someone at the top decided that no-one really needed to know anything.

## The Intelligence Conundrum

Bluffers will understand that the trouble with the intelligence process lies not so much with collection and re-tasking, but with collation, interpretation and dissemination. This is because there is simply too much data to work with. The catch is that as the data was expensive to obtain, it has to be used – even if it does mean gumming up the whole process.

For instance, while it might seem wonderful that a satellite can photograph a matchbox from ten miles high, or equally wonderful that it is possible to listen to a telephone conversation in Omsk, you can waste an awful lot of time trying to figure out:

a) What is that matchbox doing there (is it a subversive matchbox? Or significant in any way at all? Does it mean there's a shortage of lighters in the Soviet Union – and didn't we know that anyway?)

b) Is that intercepted phone conversation innocent (or is it an elaborate code, and not really between two housewives discussing where they can find sugar?)

For this we have to thank the Americans; specifically for the growth of their satellite surveillance and increased electronic eavesdropping. We also have to thank the KGB who, squirrel-like, believe that *all* information should be collected and stored.

One of the more interesting by-products of this confusion is that friendly countries spend an inordinate amount of time trying to sell data to each other. In this way they hope to recover the cost of collecting something they didn't really need in the first place. This gives the buying country even more data with which to confuse its analysts.

Bluffers should also know that French, British and Israeli intelligence differs from the Americans and

Soviets in believing that:

1. You should only concentrate on data that's obviously important.
2. The importance can often by decided by people at a fairly low level.
3. There are more important things to do than pile up data that will probably be:
    a. out of date
    b. innacurate, or
    c. defy logical analysis.

    Aside from anything else, it all cuts heavily into your social life.

One of the perpetual subjects for debate within espionage circles is 'Which is better for collecting intelligence: hardware (satellites, signal intercepting, etc.), or human beings (spies, indiscreet secretaries, etc.)?'

On the one hand, the hardware boys (CIA, NSA, GCHQ) say that their methods:

a) prove less embarrassing when found out
b) are far more accurate
c) rely heavily on computers which don't insist on unreasonable working conditions, like coffee breaks, sick leave and collections for Mavis who's getting married.

On the other hand, the traditionalists point out that:

a) electronic surveillance (satellites, intercepts) can be fooled
b) no amount of intelligence like that can ever tell ycu what people are really thinking or planning (e.g. a Soviet minister has fallen madly in love with a married Bolshoi ballet dancer)
c) all those fancy surveillance systems didn't help very much in Vietnam, Afghanistan, the Lebanon or Iran.

By and large, the logic lies with the traditionalists. However, neither argument has deterred the Soviets from launching their own space shuttle. (All shuttles are primarily intended as launchers for spy satellites by both the US and USSR.) So the bluffer can be adamant about one thing: with all that money invested in satellites, intercept stations, computers and nice new office buildings, the hardware boys will not give in without a fight. Even if their computer systems have proved vulnerable to twenty-two-year-old computer hackers with time on their hands.

The result of this information avalanche is that the few, real decision makers are:

- becoming ever more confused
- developing phobias about computers, and the curious, troll-like people who administer to them
- finding it harder to make any decisions at all.

This is the opposite of what used to happen when the only data accepted was that which helped make a previously decided policy work, or at least allowed it to fail in secret and with a certain dignity.

# INSIDE THE AGENCY

Bluffers should quickly learn to use the word 'agency'. This means understanding what it means – which is not always what you might think it means.

'The Agency' usually refers to the Central Intelligence Agency, partly because that's what it is called, partly to differentiate between the US CIA and the Korean CIA. 'An agency' is any organisation that employs espionage, and sometimes counter espionage, agents. (Note that an agency can often exist for only a single operation.) Thus while the US CIA is an agency, not all agencies are the CIA: it just seems that way.

Bluffers must also know that all agencies, including the Agency, have something in common with other types of agency (e.g. advertising, model, employment, etc.) – they all have something to sell. In the case of espionage agencies, this something is known as the 'intelligence product', which is a good business-school sort of word for information. The more and the better quality intelligence product supplied, the greater the next year's budget increase.

Counter espionage agencies do not really sell intelligence product, unless you count intelligence product that concerns itself with what spies are planning, which is not really sold, but acted upon – sometimes even in time to stop the other side's spies from spying. In fact, the better a counter espionage agency does its work, the less it will have to show for it. Obviously this is less glamorous than actually going out and discovering information to which you are not entitled, which is one reason why counter espionage agencies began spying on espionage agencies, and spying on each other, so that they, too, could have some intelligence product to sell. Or at least something, anything, to gossip about on Monday morning.

## Who Does What

Bluffers should realise that within all agencies there are:

1. Those that plan
2. Those that do.

Planners also include analysts and administrators. Doers are those who run sources. While the outside world tends to think that the doers have the more glamorous jobs, the truth is that the planners mostly hold power. They also find it easier to get life insurance.

What bluffers should do is point out that since agencies exist to gather intelligence and use networks of agents to help it do just that, it's likely that they are themselves internally organised like an espionage network, i.e. as a series of independent 'cells' (small groups), kept isolated from each other, with only a few controllers knowing who's doing what and why. Nobody will know whether you're right or wrong except those involved, and they'll never contradict you.

## Planners

Contrary to popular belief, planners may well have spent some time in the field. This is important because it allows them to:

a) accurately judge an agent's expenses
b) impress other personnel who have not.

It also allows them to look quite mean on those rare occasions when tempers flare. For who is going to argue with someone who has trod the back alleys of Prague or Hong Kong; eaten snake in Borneo; or gone missing for a week in Rio during the Carnival while theoretically arranging a defection in Peking.

On the other hand, field agents who do graduate to become administrators often become sadly embittered in the process since:

- their old friends (field agents) no longer trust them
- they discover they are junior to some paper-pusher who has never been further East than Rome. And even that was on a package tour.
- no-one is interested in hearing their best stories.

At the same time, planners are traditionally a brainy lot, much given to obscure quotations which they use when telling someone else to tell someone else to tell a particular agent to try again with his expenses, or his claim that there's an American B52 bomber on the moon.

Administrators (personnel, finance, etc.) are not always as appreciated as they feel they should be. Theirs is an unhappy lot, for agencies believe that administrators exist to keep them operating, and therefore they should do what they're told. This is entirely opposite to the bureaucrat's belief that an organisation exists to give its administrators a job, and so the organisation should do what it's told by its administrators.

## Agents

Agents work for *us*. Spies work for *them*. Bluffers should never fall into the trap of assuming that a professional respect, almost liking, exists between spies and counter-spies working for politically opposed nations. It's hard enough to get the French and British to talk politely to each other, and they are roughly meant to be on the same side. In fact there can only be one side in espionage: your own, i.e. your own country, and mostly your own agency. Or own department within your agency.

Many agents are:

- freelance
- nationals of, and resident in, another country
- people who have been bribed or blackmailed or seduced

- people who have been temporarily seconded from another department or agency.

This means that they could be a security risk. Agents do get captured and the last thing anyone wants is for the KGB to know, for instance, is how much and what sort of stationery is used in Century House. In any case it would be a little silly to have one's (presumably secret) agents seen going into headquarters, or anywhere near it. With or without a false moustache.

It is unlikely that you will ever meet an agent, or know that you've met one, but nonetheless it may be useful to know something about the breed.

Agents are often modest, unassuming sorts of people, who secretly harbour the desire to clear buildings at a single bound – if only to get away from the sources they're controlling on the one hand, and those back at head office who keep on interfering. They usually feel themselves to be distrusted by their own sources (correct), as well as their superiors (also correct). Their arcane skills include tradecraft and persuasion, dissembling and flattery, and all of a sudden having to make up one's mind on the spot. Most will fall into one of three categories:

1. Cynical and paranoid
2. Resigned and paranoid
3. Amused and paranoid.

Anyone who manages to be cynical, resigned, amused, and not too paranoid, will go far.

**Freelancers** rarely, if ever, work for the country of their birth. So it is that a German freelancer would probably only ever work for Britain, America or the Soviet Union. Nor do any self-respecting freelancers provide information that would directly damage the country of their birth. For their countries would then very probably damage them.

Freelancers are used by all espionage agencies for the simple reason that, since they are in it for the money, they should be fairly professional. Freelancers are also useful for passing unofficial messages between opposing agencies – like 'Season's Greetings', 'Happy Birthday', or 'We've just captured one of your networks and it's going to cost a mint to buy it back'.

Bluffers should know that there are also freelance agencies, often located in Switzerland. These agencies supply information on contract to organisations like the SIS, CIA, KGB, or newspapers that pride themselves on the depth of their international coverage.

Many individual freelancers are middle Europeans, marked by:

a) a well developed sense of angst
b) a well developed case of piles, caused by sitting around on cold park benches
c) an occasional sense of confusion as to who they are working for at any given moment. (It should be borne in mind that similar confusion is often felt by whichever national agency is employing the freelancer at that time.)

What with the angst, the piles and the confusion, many a freelancer's life is both short and unhappy. Their families may also find it hard to collect on their life insurance.

**Foreign resident nationals** (who may simply be sources) are considered incredibly brave if working for us, and nasty little traitors if working for them, even if both are working for idealistic reasons. The SIS and KGB try hard to convert these ideals to a need for cold, hard cash, knowing that a belief in Marx or the Magna Carta may be fleeting, but a Swiss bank account is forever. Meanwhile the CIA tend to try and convert a need for money into a belief in democracy and the American Way.

Underlining all this is the knowledge that foreigners spy on their own countries for all manner of (mixed) reasons, including:

- a desire to feel wanted and important
- a desire to do something exciting for a change
- revenge for having been passed over for promotion.

**Bribed, blackmailed or seduced** agents are often unreasonably resentful at being any or all of these, which you could consider is a little ungrateful of them since it's probably their own fault in the first place. Handlers never miss an opportunity to remind them how lucky they are to work for an agency more than happy to forget their indiscretions, perhaps even to feed their greed, or encourage their excesses – just so long as they do what they're told. Bluffers should appreciate that agents like these are living (well, for a time anyway) proof of the famous dictum: 'Everyone has his or her price. And it isn't always money.'

Bribed, blackmailed or seduced agents are not always the easiest to work with. Many give way to flashes of temper, or floods of tears. This is usually intensely embarrassing and liable to attract attention, neither of which is good for business. In addition, a flawed character is a flawed character, and may attract other agencies who have also become aware of an individual's weakness.

**Temporarily seconded agents** aren't easily defined. They can include:

a) people from another government department, or friendly agency

b) civilians taken on for a specific job.

In neither case will they be used as other agents are. It's unlikely, for example, that someone on loan from the CIA would be given access to a source who is a member of the

Soviet Politburo. Instead, they will be used as couriers, say, or bodyguards. Or for those occasional jobs that must have no official or even unofficial involvement with the agency. This latter instance can involve civilians being used, and quite often the civilians themselves will not know that a certain agency is their ultimate employer. (Not that this will cut much ice with the other side if they're caught.) Bluffers should be aware of the rumours that certain private security firms are used in just this way.

Temporarily seconded agents are often lonely, financially hard up, and bored. Getting involved with an agency gives them:

- the emotional security of being needed by an organisation
- tax free income (although one of the more pressing arguments in Britain is whether agents' ex gratia payments should be subject to VAT. And if so, should SIS be VAT registered)
- plenty of opportunity for free travel.

It is understood that this type of working relationship relies on the maxim: 'Give 'em what they want. Give 'em what they need. And they'll be loyal – until a better offer comes along.'

# How To Handle Agency Staff:

**Analysts** should be shown the respect due to someone who knows how to get to Perm from Rostov without changing at Moscow.
*Win over by*: agreeing that the recent fall in the price of tin probably will result in a trade war between Iceland and Indonesia over new markets for pumice stone.
*Dominate by*: proving that all of Indonesia's pumice stone is actually earmarked for Japan, where it will be used to manufacture large, decoy whales.

**Planners** should be shown the respect due to someone who probably understands Chaos mathematical theory, and certainly seems to run operations on that basis.
*Win over by*: being able to quote Dante in Aramaic.
*Dominate by*: taking truffle sandwiches to work.

**Administrators** should be shown the sort of fawning respect they secretly long for.
*Win over by*: assuming they know everything that happens within their agency.
*Dominate by*: giving the impression you really work for an organisation so secret that even the agency hasn't heard of it.

**Agents (Field Personnel)** should not just be shown respect, but actually respected. They could cause considerable harm to your health.
*Win over by*: establishing as quickly as possible that you pose no threat to them in any way; a vacant expression and the tendency to drool gently will serve admirably.
*Dominate*: DON'T EVEN TRY.

# BRITISH INTELLIGENCE

Everyone is aware that, in Britain, SIS is the espionage agency, while MI5 is the counter espionage agency. However, the bluffer should be aware that SIS does not spend all its time running spies. It also spends a good deal, possibly most, of its time analysing data obtained from overt sources, like the Omsk Evening Chronicle. Naturally, this information is not in itself secret. But SIS's interest in it very definitely is.

SIS is also concerned with the KGB, and what it is planning. As is MI5. This means that SIS and MI5 sometimes duplicate their activities, a situation that may lead to recriminations over the biscuits at joint conferences.

Again, in theory SIS only operates abroad, while MI5 operates at home. Except that neither could do their job, or enlarge their empires, if this was the case. So MI5 does operate abroad if it's in connection with something that's happening at home. While SIS can operate at home if it's to do with something happening abroad. Both blame each other when confusion results.

## SIS

SIS, as most will know, stands for Secret Intelligence Service. It used to be called MI6, but that made it sound junior to MI5, which was generally felt to be a bad thing (except, of course, by MI5). However, what others won't necessarily know is whether its name means:

a) the Intelligence is secret
b) the Service is secret.

In fact, both are true. The Intelligence is secret because

no-one should know what the SIS is interested in, or what they've got. The Service is secret because no-one should know where or what it is.

Of course, as the bluffer can point out:

a) a child of ten could probably figure out what the SIS was interested in
b) most readers of spy novels know that it is based in Century House in South London, but that the only thing that happens there for certain, is post mortems.

Note that the SIS displays a certain charming modesty in not having large signs outside its headquarters saying 'SIS Head Office', unlike the CIA and KGB. And that it's likely the SIS uses other buildings and not all of them are grey, government blocks pretending to be an offshoot of the Ministry of Agriculture, Food and Fisheries.

In fact, if you ever suspect an office block is housing an organisation like SIS or MI5, there is one sure way to find out: walk past the entrance several times in a few minutes; even loiter a little, be seen to make notes. Then, if:

– you're suddenly approached by a muscular looking sort of chap, who claims to have known you at Oxford, it's probably SIS
– if someone presses a gun in your back, it's probably MI5
– if a stranger asks you to complete an IQ test, it's probably the CIA. Or the Scientologists. Or someone selling life insurance
– if you're run over by a Lada, it's probably the KGB.

The operative word with the SIS is 'Service'. SIS personnel are highly motivated by a sense of noblesse oblige. So are the KGB in their own way, which is why the Soviet Union has all sorts of schools designed to develop the sort of noblesse that Britain produces without even thinking. The CIA would like to have their own noblesse, but nowadays most graduates from Harvard, Yale or Princeton become insider dealers on Wall Street. Instead the CIA operates on the basis of loyalty to:

a) democracy
b) the current US President
c) the American Dream.

SIS personnel are nothing if not subtle. MI5 would probably say devious. This is because:

- SIS work attracts people with a subtle turn of mind
- SIS work fosters a subtle turn of mind
- If you don't learn how to be subtle, you won't last long in SIS.

Deviousness often shows in SIS-speak, an elliptical way of talking in which:

  - nothing very much is said, especially to outsiders (i.e. anyone who is not a member of SIS)
  - quite a long time is spent in not saying much
  - pauses, raised eyebrows, half smiles, etc. are every bit as important as (probably more than) actual words.

For bluffers wishing to develop SIS-speak for themselves, the rules are fairly simple:

1. Never state, only suggest.
2. Never challenge, only "raise a minor point that may have some bearing on the matter".
3. Never let the other person know what you're really thinking.
4. Give the impression you know more than you do.
5. If you're forced into asking a direct question, give the impression that you already know the answer, and that this is actually some kind of intelligence or loyalty test.
6. If forced into answering a question, keep the answer to one or two curt syllables.

7. Never raise your voice. But you may show sadness, hurt, concern or exasperation.

It is worth remembering that this method of talking owes much to the fact that SIS personnel never know, can never know, whether the person they're talking to is secretly working for the CIA, KGB, MI5, the Prime Minister of the day, and possibly all four at the same time.

## Who Runs It

Nominally the SIS is responsible to the Foreign Secretary. This pleases the Foreign and Commonwealth Office (FCO) no end, since it likes to think it controls SIS. The SIS is happy to go along with this fiction because it means that SIS personnel are not banished to the Staff Canteen in British Embassies abroad. Ultimately it is the Prime Minister who is head of SIS, or rather carries the can when anything goes seriously wrong. But no Prime Minister or Foreign Secretary ever truly wants to know what SIS is up to. If they did, how could they keep a straight face when meeting foreign leaders? Nor is SIS always that keen on politicians knowing too much about its activities, since:

a) they might say 'no'
b) they might come up with the occasional crazy idea of their own
c) they just might try to use SIS for their own political ends.

In practice, SIS answers to a small clearing house of permanent civil servants, which is probably the only group in Britain that has a rough idea of what both SIS and MI5 are doing. And whether they are doing it to each other.

# How To Pretend To Belong To SIS

Some people have wanted to become espionage agents all their lives; have even gone to the trouble of:

a) becoming fluent in three foreign languages,
b) joining certain clubs
c) working as a foreign correspondent for an up-market newspaper
d) bribing their way into the MCC;

without so much as having been approached.

The point is that whereas the CIA advertises for permanent staff, all the other agencies can only be joined by invitation. And no-one knows what the criteria for selection are.

However, if you are ever lucky enough to be:

- called for a job interview with an export agency that is unclear about what it exports
- interviewed by someone whose name doesn't appear in any telephone directory, anywhere, or whose name doesn't correspond to the initials on his briefcase
- interviewed by a retired colonel whose entry in *Who's Who* doesn't mention what he's been doing for the past fifteen years

the chances are that you are being head-hunted by SIS or MI5.

If you do succeed in bluffing your way into an agency remember that you're there for life. No-one ever really leaves intelligence or security work. Indeed, it is very hard to be sacked from, say, SIS or MI5. People worry that you might turn nasty and Tell All to the KGB. Or worse, the French. Or even worse, members of Her Majesty's Opposition. If you don't succeed in becoming permanent staff, you may well be asked to help out occasionally. And while this can be fun, you must know that it often takes a long time to get your expenses back.

Assuming therefore that you simply want to give the impression that you already belong, you are faced with a choice:

1. give the impression of being head office staff, or
2. give the impression of being a field agent.

NB: No bluffer would ever want to give the impression of working for the KGB as a field agent, or in any capacity, come to that, for as a pretend (or real) field agent you will have to:

a) talk English with a marked Dutch accent, which is how a Russian usually sounds when he's trying to talk with a Canadian accent, which is what most KGB field agents try to do
b) use an American Express card for absolutely everything.

Nor is it any easier to be a pretend (or real) CIA field agent, since you would be required to:

a) carry a portable satellite receiving dish at all times
b) talk English with a Cockney accent that sounds like Dick van Dyke in *Mary Poppins*.

Any, or all of these may well make you conspicuous, insolvent, or an object of ridicule amongst your friends.

Bluffers should also be aware of the inherent problem in pretending to belong to any agency: people may believe you – even those you would rather did not. For example, if you successfully induce the suspicion that you are a member of:

- the SIS, MI5 may well try to recruit you
- the KGB, you will be faced with a long delay at Malaga airport
- the CIA, you will probably be denied entrance to Spain itself.

Whether you opt to bluff as head office staff or a field agent, you must learn to develop certain behavioural characteristics common to both, e.g.

1. A refusal to sit with you back to the door
2. Sudden unexplained absences
3. An obsession with some wildly inappropriate subject, like toad-spotting.

Once you have perfected these basic ploys, you may begin to add on those that are particular to one or the other, as follows:

**The Field Agent**:

- Receive mysterious phone calls
- Exhibit occasional symptoms of extreme mental and physical stress, such as diving under a table when the landlord yells 'time', then claiming you were searching for a dropped peanut.
- absent mindedly pay for a round of drinks with foreign (Eastern block) currency, insisting it dates from your last holiday, when everyone knows you were supposed to be walking in Scotland.
- refuse to get involved in a physical fight (the reason being, of course, that you dare not expose your cover by felling your opponent with a single blow).

**The Head Office Worker**:

- Make mysterious telephone calls.
- Drop a few esoteric facts about espionage into the conversation, such as:
  a) the Byzantine Empire boasted an entire ministry devoted to espionage and internal security
  b) Marco Polo was the Republic of Venice's best known spy
  c) Akhbar (Indian Moghul ruler) employed four thousand secret agents and received an intelligence digest every day

d) British military intelligence was given a citation for looking after its carrier pigeons so well in the First World War.

   But never mention any of these facts when espionage itself is being talked about. Instead, wait until talk turns – in this instance – to Turkey, India, Italy or birds.

- If asked whether you belong, dismiss the question by saying "I'd really rather not talk about that if, you don't mind." Be seen later to note down the number of his or her car.
- Know how many zlotys there are to the pound.
- Know what a zloty is.

Bluffers should also keep in mind that, whoever you are purporting to be, should the conversation ever turn to how SIS justifies its existence (usually expressed by a monetarist, a Trotskyite, or someone from MI5) the ideal rejoinder is that SIS has passed the point of needing to justify its existence. Say it is just a strange fact of contemporary life. Note that this should be said in a humorous, self-deprecating sort of way. And should anyone have the temerity to suggest that espionage is a total waste of time, you should:

- stare blankly at the culprit
- permit yourself, after a few seconds, a minute and sardonic smile
- murmur something to the effect that you hadn't realised there was an expert present
- then take no further part in the discussion. Instead stare distantly into space as if reliving past triumphs or disasters.

You must note that the following would be going too far in the attempt to establish your credentials:

a) lurking anywhere (officially discouraged by SIS except for middle European agents who know no other means of movement)
b) limping
c) wearing trench coats and slouch hats (unless female)
d) wearing a twin set and pearls (unless male, and bluffing in the role of a traitor)
e) referring to the CIA as 'the cousins', which is now considered passé
f) referring to the 'Kay Jee Bee'. The current pronounciation is Kar Gay Bay; you can also be really fashionable and refer to the Kar Gay Bears.
g) claiming to understand the plots of le Carré; aside from anything else, your friends will vanish lest you begin to explain what Smiley really meant.

## MI5

MI5 used to stand for Military Intelligence (section) 5. This dates back to the days when all security and intelligence work was effectively handled by the military or the police. Bluffers should know that the major difference today is that many MI5 personnel are ex, rather than serving, military personnel, while the police element is to be found in Special Branch. MI5 is also variously known as 'five', Box 500 (its official London postal address); Leconfield House (its one-time main London headquarters); or 'the funnies' (usually used by people who have something to fear). In similar vein, MI5 personnel often refer to SIS as 'friends', a neat piece of sarcasm if ever there was one.

Until the draft legislation of November 1988, MI5 was in the happy position of not existing. And as it didn't exist, no-one knew:

a) what it was supposed to do
b) how it did it
c) where it did it from
d) how successful it was –

all of which led to much envy from other government departments, who only wished they could be in the same idyllic state. Today, most people are aware that MI5 has the responsibility of protecting us from:

- espionage
- sabotage
- subversion
- terrorism.

You should note that the first three are only crimes when they threaten the security of the State, and that the State decides when security is in fact being threatened. You could claim that this is because there are occasions when only the State *can* know when its security is being threatened.

Of the threats that MI5 guard us all against, espionage is straightforward; sabotage and terrorism, self-explanatory. The problem area is subversion, since few people know exactly what it means. It is probably best to think of subversion as 'going too far'-though not necessarily as far as sabotage or terrorism, and usually without the associated noise, blood and mayhem. It can also be the attempt to persuade another person to be disloyal to, or commit an illegal act against, his or her own country; or any one of the following:

– encouraging strikes for strictly political purposes
– organising non-violent demonstrations
– being unkind about the Royal Family.

There are three considerations as to whether an act is subversive enough to warrant MI5's interest:

1. The intention (Is the planned modest demonstration just a rehearsal for a later riot?)
2. The act itself (How damaging is it really?)
3. The result (Does the media demand that Something Must Be Done?).

Bluffers should never forget that MI5 holds the view that everyone is a little bit subversive to begin with. Remember, too, how concern with subversion works, say, in relation to legitimate political movements. For example, CND activists are often incensed (or possible secretly delighted) at the thought of MI5 having them under surveillance. Those same activists would probably be mortified to know that MI5 is not concerned so much with them, as with others who might attempt to turn CND into something violent. However, if all the people who claimed that MI5 were watching them were to be believed, MI5 would need a work force of some twenty thousand people ... instead of the little over two thousand it actually possesses.

## How It Operates

Within MI5 there are separate sections dealing with:

- the Soviet Union and Warsaw Pact
- the IRA
- other terrorist groups, e.g. PLO, Black September, and possibly lager louts
- security vetting
- security of classified or commercially important industrial secrets (particularly in relation to the Defence industry)
- training of friendly foreigners.

There are others but, by and large, these are the most interesting.

## Vetting

Anyone who comes into contact with classified information must be vetted, i.e. judged:

a) not to be unstable
b) not to bear more sympathy for a foreign country (any foreign country) than his or her own
c) not to be open to blackmail.

There are two points the bluffer should note:

1. Vetting only confirms what you have not done. Not what you might do.
2. Blackmail used to include things that you should be ashamed of. Now it tends to include only things you might go to prison for.

A good deal of the vetting process is carried out by ex-Army officers or retired policemen. If you are ever vetted yourself, you should be wary of simple sounding questions like 'Do you drink black coffee?' (he's trying to discover if you suffer from hangovers, i.e. do you drink). Unfortunately there will also be one which will damn you whatever you answer, e.g. 'Do you like girls?' (If yes, and you may be a paedophile, if no, you are a sitting duck for blackmail.) Vetting personnel have little or no sense of humour. On the other hand, they are almost impossible to shock. It will automatically be assumed you're guilty of something, so it's best to admit to some small peccadillo, merely to put their minds at rest.

## Industrial or Commercial Security

As commercial firms discover, as soon as they possess anything that is judged vital to the country, it often seems to become part owned by the country. This means that obscure men from MI5 ('No, I won't mention my name. And this meeting never took place, right?') descend on the firm in order to make sure the secret won't get stolen by:

a) a foreign power
b) a foreign company
c) Japan.

(Japan is in a league of its own since it poses no military threat, but its businesses exist in part to carry out Japanese foreign policy.)

Visits like these from MI5 are a time of deep frustration all round. MI5 can't believe that civilians can't see the necessity for locking typewriter ribbons, word processor discs, etc. in a secure safe and swallowing the key. Civilians can't understand the need for a number of men called 'Smith' who insist on knowing what the office cleaners' great grandfather did in the Boer War.

## Training of Friendly Foreigners

Bluffers know that Britain maintained her Empire largely by setting up a ruling, indigenous clique in her colonies, and inviting them, at least once, to meet Queen Victoria. Today, Britain helps maintain her influence by training foreign equivalents of MI5 (as do other Western countries, such as the US and France).

Britain, however, is well aware that foreigners do not always remain friendly. So training courses are unlikely to give too much away – a little basic draw-locking perhaps. Or possibly primary card indexing and elementary 'trailing'. The result is that any foreign policeman who insists on driving on the wrong side of the road in his own country; or re-indexing his own country's suspects in English; or showing a tendency to lock everything inside his desk, and then lose the key ... such a man was probably trained in Britain.

## How To Handle MI5 Personnel

Ex-military (regimental types, slightly shaggy haired with a predilection for chukka boots; favourite habitat, Wiltshire or Dorset).

*How to handle*:

- grow a small, toothbrush moustache (women included)
- practise standing to attention
- wax lyrical about labradors.

Ex-policeman (two-piece suit with Rotary pin in the lapel, white shirt, highly polished black shoes, and a light, striped polyester tie).

*How to handle*:

- refer to suspects as 'chummy'
- be overheard wishing that everyone could wear uniform at least once a year
- brush your shoes every hour, on the hour.

Home-grown MI5 (looks like anyone: be careful).

*How to handle*:

- let it be known that you're close, personal friends with a particularly violent South London gang.

# TRADECRAFT

Tradecraft encompasses all the art, the skills, the tricks of the trade. Everyone working in espionage or counter espionage in any capacity is inordinately proud of 'tradecraft'. It makes them somehow a little different from everyone else. It also fools many people that they are learning a skill which will be of use if they ever return to the civilian world.

Bluffers should know that while the names of various tradecraft techniques may differ from country to country, agency to agency, the principles remain the same. Tradecraft concerns how one goes about spying without being:

a) caught
b) killed
c) exposed in the Sunday newspapers.

Books by people like Len Deighton and Ted Allbeury are full of all those little words and phrases that differentiate between the amateur and the professional, so you should concentrate on aspects of tradecraft that are not usually covered in spy novels, usually because:

– the writer doesn't know about them
– the writer doesn't want to admit to knowing about them
– they have no place in the plot.

You should know for instance:

- The best way to approach a clandestine meeting that you think may have been compromised (i.e. the wrong side knows about it). You don't. Someone disposable is sent instead.
- The number of people you need to follow one suspect in a city like London for 24 hours a day. At least ten, plus three cars at any given time; cars that are changed every four hours – one of which will look like a taxi or minicab.

But, more importantly, you should know about source handling, as done by agents. This is the most necesssary skill of all. Few people outside the world of espionage and counter espionage know anything about it.

## Source Handling

Source handling is the art of dealing with someone who has information you need, someone who doesn't want to give you the information, or someone who doesn't know that you want the information in the first place. Sources, then, are anyone or anything that has information that you want. They can be:

**passive** – not aware that they hold any information or how important it is. (A document or piece of machinery would come into this category – lacking, as they do, self awareness. So would a clerk or copy typist.)

**active** – very much aware of how important they are (e.g. the average private secretary).

**conscious** – aware that they are giving you information.

**unconscious** – unaware that you are anything other than a drinking companion who can, on occasions, be a sympathetic listener to tales of what went wrong in the office.

Many agencies consider that passive is the same as unconscious, and active the same as conscious. But you must insist on the differences between the four. It's far more subtle. It's also more accurate. Point out that the ideal source is both passive and unconscious. For example, a document found in the pocket (and swiftly copied before being returned) of a drunken member of the KGB who has passed out in his own home in Moscow.

Sadly such cases are rare. Usually most sources are:

- suffering from an inflated opinion of their own value
- determined to be loved for their own sake, and not just for the information they possess
- convinced that everyone is against them
- full of guilt
- greedy
- bent on some sort of revenge
- surly and resentful since they've been blackmailed into becoming sources in the first instance.

You should also know that all information coming from a source is graded according to:

a) the reliability of the source
b) the probability that the information is correct
c) the reliability of the source handler, i.e. agent.

This is another way of saying that no-one trusts anyone or anything. Even if, say, a high ranking KGB officer made contact with SIS and offered to tell all because he had embraced truth, democracy and the Changing of the Guard, his information would always be suspect. At least by the British, who tend to be a little more cynical, or practical, than their American counterparts. But not quite as cynical as the French.

So, theoretically, sources come in several different types, and you can take your pick from:

1. Those who are seeking ego satisfaction
2. Those who are seeking solace
3. Those who need status
4. Those who need money
5. Those who need the stimulus
6. Those who are naturally devious
7. Those who have been 'persuaded' (e.g. blackmailed)
8. Those who genuinely think they are doing the Right Thing.

Bluffers will realise that many sources are combinations of two of more of the above. The good ones may well harbour a deep grievance; the bad ones may well exhibit a touching desire to do something noble. Handling them can be very difficult indeed. Note also that most sources will, at some time:

- produce photos of their families
- become quite tearful
- lie over silly little things, like their own name
- sweat a lot.

Any source who does not do any of the above is probably a plant. Any source who does is either looking for reassurance or more money. Go easy on the money, but give as much re-assurance as you like.

The KGB reduce everything to a basic level (cash). Even if someone walks into the Soviet Embassy swearing blind that they've been a secret Marxist for years, at some time the KGB will insist that they accept money for their services. The Americans will want to believe that their source truly believes in democracy, and reward the source handsomely for doing so, while the British will try to get away with as much as they can. (NB: bluffers must know that the KGB are motivated by:

a) loyalty to Mother Russia
b) loyalty to the KGB
c) access to special shops

in that order. Ideology doesn't really come into it. The most that senior KGB officers will admit to these days is a sneaking regard for socialism, having recognised all its faults.)

Source handlers, therefore, are those people in direct contact with an active source, and who may or may not be the person who recruited the source in the first place – even though the source will not always know that he or she has been recruited.

It is true that an emotional bond can form between the source and source handler. The KGB insist upon it, but then the Russians tend to be much more emotional about things. However, the biggest obstacle to successful source handling lies with the 'experts' at head office. Bluffers should take account of the fact that a combination of creeping bureaucracy and 'jobs for specialists' policy in head office has resulted in a plethora of psychologists (mostly behavioural, always obscure), sociologists, and various hangers on. All are desk men and all are determined that a source should be handled in accordance with their superior knowledge. This makes them feel involved and important. Source handlers quickly learn to disregard the wilder flights of fancy produced by these armchair warriors, as in: "The key word to use in your dealings with this source is 'strudel'. His psychological profile indicates that it will remind him of his childhood and help develop an emotional dependency. If possible, carry some strudel with you when you next meet." The source handler goes chuckling about his work, secure in the knowledge that this particular source is relying on him to keep quiet about certain indiscretions that could get him a long prison sentence, and is in any case on a strict diet.

It is axiomatic of source handling that all sources will lie. It is also axiomatic that all source handlers will:

a. appear to believe the lie
b. appear to disbelieve the truth.

It is vital to retain the whip hand, for the essence of source handling is control. As a good source handler you must never lose it; never allow yourself to sympathise too much with the source; never allow the source to realise quite how useful the information is (or isn't).

At the same time, it is essential to make the source feel that he or she is important. Techniques for doing this will differ from country to country. The Soviets are great believers in presenting their sources with medals and promoting them within the KGB. Naturally the source never gets to wear the medals, or his KGB uniform, until he runs to Moscow where he can mix with other ex-KGB sources and compare medals and insignia of rank. The British believe in letting the source come to slow realisation of his own usefulness. Having done so, the source will try hard to get his or her handler to admit that the information provided is essential. This you will deny, but with a certain lack of conviction, i.e. allow the source the hope that he or she really *is* a valued and trusted member of the team. This particular approach of the British is because a source aware of his own importance always costs more money. On those occasions when a source genuinely knows how valuable he is, and wants to be paid accordingly, the British have one basic ploy: sell him to the Americans.

The rules therefore are:

1. Make the source feel important and appreciated, until such time as the information begins to dry up, at which point
2. Threaten him or her with exposure.
3. Appear to accept their stated motivations, even though you know they are lying through their teeth.
4. Never ask the source for anything terribly important in the beginning; work up to it slowly, until it's too late for them to pull out.
5. Whenever you have to bring pressure to bear on the source, it is never your idea. It is always at the instruction of your superiors 'back at the office'.

Meetings with sources must always be held in places that will cause the least suspicion, or the least embarrassment to source and handler if caught. For those reasons, it is never a good idea to meet in:

a) the source's own embassy (there might be some slight difficulty getting out)
b) the middle of a park (difficult to tell if you've been followed)
c) an underground car park (too depressing)
d) a gentleman's lavatory (too smelly).

Instead, meetings should be held in places where you can both hide in the crowd, such as:

- concerts
- long distance trains
- passenger ferries
- airports
- sports stadia
- turkish baths (unless your source is gay and you are not).

It is considered to be a little amateur to ask a source if he or she was "followed on the way here". If they had been followed they would either not have noticed, or they would have noticed and gone somewhere quiet to wring their hands. A smart source handler will always try to reach a meeting early. This gives you a chance to try and figure out if that dog in the vicinity has a microphone tied around its neck, whether that small child playing so innocently is actually a killer dwarf, or to enjoy the soccer game for a bit before your source arrives to tell you tearfully why he's failed yet again to get what you wanted.

All source handlers who are also agents will need some sort of cover – a reason for being in that particular part of the world at that particular time. This often means a false identity and can cause problems. It is extremely difficult to assume a foreign identity, as the US discovered to their cost when they sent hundreds of agents into the Soviet

Union in the 1950s. Being able to pass oneself off as a foreign national means knowing:

a) all the 'current' jokes
b) all the regional differences
c) all the familiarity built up over a lifetime, often without being aware of it.

The Soviets discovered this long ago, which is why so many of their agents in the UK or US claimed to be Canadian. At the time:

- it was easy to get a Canadian passport (all you needed was proof that you were in fact alive)
- Canadians were regarded by the rest of the world as being mostly harmless
- both Russians and Canadians know a great deal about snow, and a few minutes' description of a major blizzard would lull the most suspicious mind into a sense of security.

Today, it is generally accepted that a correct false identity is one that:

- admits you to be a foreign national
- allows you to travel around a great deal
- gives you good reason for appearing inquisitive.

In other words, an identity that gives a reasonable explanation for your sometimes agent-like behaviour. The following would be ideal:

travelling salesman
journalist
Embassy or consular official
author
member of a trade delegation
tourist.

If you have to pass yourself off as a foreign national certain elementary rules must be followed. For example, if you are contemplating a short trip to East Germany, be sure to:

a) get rid of all your British coins
b) know the names of the East German athletes who won gold medals at the last Olympics
c) change into East German clothes
d) sneer secretly at any passing Russian
e) insist on meeting your source as close to your escape route as possible – whatever those at head office have said.

All this assumes that you can speak fluent German with an appropriate accent.

The other major problem concerning complete changes of identity is that it can become very confusing. Just as the double agent (working for two sides) or triple agent (pretending to work for both sides, actually only working for one) often ends up forgetting who he really is working for (as may his employers, who will solve the problem with a little fatal accident), so, too, is the agent faced with the question 'Who am I supposed to be today?' Worse, the characteristics of one persona may inadvertently appear in another. Obviously this all becomes somewhat of a strain. Retired agents who have lived such an adventurous life are fond of asking other retired agents 'Do you know who I am?'; 'Do you know what I did?' They are not boasting. they are genuinely trying to find out.

## Cryptology

Bluffers must know that cryptology is the science of coding printed, verbal or photographic information in such a way that no-one without the code can understand it, or breaking that same code. Even if cryptology were made simple, less than one person in a million would probably understand it. As bluffers will realise, the principle behind the Enigma device had been around a long, long time, but that didn't make it any easier to crack.

Nowadays, codes and ciphers are computer generated using elaborate formulae. Scientists then devise new ways of cracking those same codes, using other formulae. While this may lead to a Nobel prize, it makes life difficult for espionage agencies. Sadly (for the hardware boys) it seems that the only truly secure methods are:

1. the one time pad (a randomly generated code, printed out as a series of only-to-be-used-once figures corresponding to letters of the alphabet)
2. the old 'book code', where two people (and only ever two) agree on a book, preferably easily available. Messages are made by either selecting individual words or letters from different pages, and then sending the location instructions, e.g. 33.2.4.2. (i.e. page 33, second para, fourth line, second word).

Unfortunately both these methods are:

a) a little cumbersome
b) time consuming
c) likely to produce sneers from people who claim to understand Probability and Set Theory. Not to mention Boolean algebra and Prime Numbers.

The main problem with all codes/ciphers is that the mere possession of them is more than enough to make even the most unimaginative security policeman, or landlady, deeply suspicious. And while it's true that they can be hidden, it becomes a little awkward if every time you want to send a message, you have to:

- unscrew a can of shaving foam or talcum powder, fish about with your fingers to find the microfilm, and then clean it
- prise up a floor board
- spend hours looking for *the* book, only to find it's been borrowed without asking by a friend.

The other problem is that codes and ciphers are extremely complicated, one false step and the whole thing can look like gibberish, which is very trying when you're in a cold sweat because men in uniforms (or raincoats) are lurking outside your house. In addition, very complex codes need fairly large devices both to send and receive them, devices that are usually found in the basements of embassies, and an agent can't spend all his or her time popping in to an Embassy on the pretext of acquiring travel brochures.

Similar strictures apply to transmitters, all very wonderful in theory, but in practice a dead giveaway if they're found. Nor will your explanation that it's really a special radio designed to pick up Radio 4 or Radio Moscow or Voice of America, go down very well. Whatever the case, a bluffer can be certain that any agent given a set of codes or ciphers plus the equipment to use them will only be a courier or 'cut-out'. No important, in-place source would ever be compromised by being asked to use techniques and equipment that have the word 'spy' written all over them.

## How to Work for a Foreign Agency

In order to be approached by, say, the CIA or KGB you should be able to give the impression that you:

1. know certain things they want to know
2. are basically loyal to your own country
3. can probably get tickets for important first nights.

Remember, however, that no-one really trusts an ideological agent, since;

- espionage personnel are motivated by love of country, which is not always to do with love of democracy, etc.
- ideological agents can become a trifle embittered, as when they discover that:

a. life in the USSR is not exactly a paradise for the workers
b. life in the USA can be a little shrill and dangerous unless you hold medical insurance
c. life in Britain is difficult unless you're wearing the correct tie.

This means that you should at some time ask for money. But it is unwise to ask for:

- too much, less they think you greedy
- too little, less they think you amateur.

Prices vary, but in principle, your payment should have a direct relation to the punishment you could expect from your own country if it catches you working against it. Thus, in Britain, the scale would be:

| *Sentence if caught* | *Payment* |
|---|---|
| Life imprisonment* | £75-100,000 |
| Twenty years* | £50,000 plus |
| Ten years* | £20,000 plus |
| Five years | £10,000 plus |
| Two years | £5,000 plus |
| Probation | Luncheon vouchers |

*with hard labour, add 10 per cent.

If the penalty of being caught is death (and for treason it can still be, in the UK), you should insist on:

- a payment in gold of at least £150,000
- a Swiss bank account
- your funeral expenses as an end of contract bonus.

As bluffers will realise, it is sensible to confine your activities to those little jobs that will, if you're caught, get you a prison sentence of between two and ten years – so that you can get out on parole after one to five. For while jobs in this category (often simply passing messages from one person to another) do not pay as highly as the more glamorous sort (stealing documents, say), you can do several in the course of a month. In fact at this level you will be able to become a true freelance, often working for many different agencies. But only one at a time, mind.

The snag is how you get to the attention of the foreign agency in the first instance; that is to say, how to get them to approach you. They will undoubtedly become suspicious of any overt approaches on your part, assuming you:

a) might be an agent provocateur
b) might be an 'intelligence nuisance' (someone dazzled by the supposed riches and glamour who has little to sell other than the aliens at the bottom of the garden.

So unless you are in some sort of sensitive job (with access to secret information) and are known to be desperately hard up and at odds with your employers, the best idea is probably to join one of those friendship clubs where you will be surrounded by MI5 agents, intelligence nuisances, and people genuinely interested in friendship between countries who are tolerated for the sake of authenticity.

Bluffers should abandon all thoughts about being recruited by a glamorous, sexy spy. This was once one of the favourite gambits of the KGB until they realised that visiting businessmen had figured out the best way of enjoying their stay in Moscow was to appear lonely, or to appear more important than they really were. Nor were the incriminating photographs of much use, since everyone now knows that such evidence can easily be forged. (It can't in fact, but the fact that everyone thinks so, including businessmen's wives, makes it far less useful.)

Of course, there still remains the homosexual 'honey trap' (recruitment by sex) but even here an effective response has proved to be:

a. I was drugged
b. it's a forgery
c. I'm about to join the Gay Liberation Front.

# GLOSSARY

**Adviser(s)** – Either bureaucratic or military thugs. Neither their advice nor their presence can be safely ignored.

**Agency** – Collection of devious personalities dedicated to preventing the left hand knowing the right hand exists.

**Agent** – Someone who thinks he or she knows who they're really working for. Sometimes, they might even be correct.

**Alibi** – Your excuse for being found lurking outside a top-secret establishment with a camera and telephoto lens.

**ASIO** – Australian Security Intelligence Organisation, the Aussie secret service, unique since the name actually describes the function.

**Bad guys** – Sometimes the other side. More often, those on your side who disapprove of what you're doing.

**Beyond salvage** – An operation or individual that's been so compromised, you simply forget about them and go on to something else.

**BritMilInt** – British Military Intelligence. Mostly Army, although the RAF are allowed to play if they shave off their moustaches, as are the Royal Navy, since they have all the best jokes.

**Bug** – The planting of listening devices of various degrees of sophistication, all of which are guaranteed to stop working at the crucial time.

**Burn** – To expose a freelance or double agent, or even one of your own.

**Buy** – Pay good money for information you could probably have found in the *Scientific American* for free.

**Cage** – Physically secure communications room (i.e. impervious to bugging. (But the staff aren't impervious to either bribery or blackmail.)

**Cell** – Independent intelligence or espionage group that only knows its immediate upwards and downwards contacts, at least, in theory.

**Character deterioration** – Annoying phenomena whereby agents-in-place tend to go to pieces under the strain and start doing strange things, the feeble minded wimps.

**Code word** – A pretentious or juvenile word or phrase used to refer to something that everyone knows about anyway.

**COMSEC** – Communications Security, i.e. a make work programme for the computer industry.

**Counter agent** – Someone used to stop *them* finding out about you. Or what you're up to. Many an espionage operations ends with the two main protagonists giving up and going home, but forgetting to tell their respective counter agents who are still slugging it out together. This is afterwards referred to as a 'breakdown in communications'.

**Courier** – Someone employed solely to carry information from point A to point B, preferably without knowing where or from whom it originated; what it is, and who's going to be using it. Not surprisingly, couriers tend to sulk a lot, especially when caught.

**Cousins** – Originally SIS-speak for the CIA. Increasingly used to refer to any American organisation.

**Cover** – Your reason, ranging from a legitimate job to a false identity, for being able to hide the fact that you work for an intelligence/espionage organisation.

**Cowboy** – Someone who's let the business go to his or her head; or someone who acts in a particularly amateur and heavy-handed manner.

**Cut-out** – Person of little significance used purely as a link so that more important people won't be seen together. Also, equally insignificant person responsible for passing information from one courier to another. Cut-outs should never, ever, know anything about what they're doing. When caught, they tend to sulk even more than couriers do.

**Dead letter drop** – Somewhere one person can hide information so that it can later be picked up by another, neither ever seeing each other.

**Deep cover** – An agent or source with such a good cover that he or she has probably forgotten they're supposed to be working for you.

**Defector-in-place** – Someone who wants to defect, but has been persuaded to hang on for 'just a little longer' in order to provide valuable information. (And as that 'little longer' stretches into years, character deterioration invariably sets in.)

**Double agent** – Someone who's working for you although apparently working for them. Or is he?

**Disinformation** – Carefully spread false rumour close enough to the truth to cause all sorts of problems.

**Echo** – Evidence that the other side has bought the disinformation programme hook, line and sinker.

**Elint** – Electronic intelligence, i.e. information gained from scanning the electro-magnetic spectrum.

**Factor X** – The ability some intelligence organisations have of being in the right place at the right time. Known disparagingly by the CIA as 'lucky', especially when talking about the SIS.

**Flop** – Action of an individual changing sides.

**Good guys** – Anyone who's in favour of what you're doing. Anyone at all.

**GRU** – Chief Intelligence Directorate, General Staff; Soviet military intelligence subordinate to the KGB inasmuch as it reports to the General Staff, whereas the **KGB** – Komitat Gosundarst-vennoi Bezopasnosti (Committee for State Security) – reports directly to the Defence Council and the Politburo itself.

**Heavies** – Those who do whatever dirty work needs doing.

**Humint** – Human intelligence, i.e. information gained from a human source.

**Intelligence nuisance** – Someone who's always claiming to have vital information, but never does.

**In-place source** – One who is in the right place. If British in the USSR, desperately trying to get out; if Soviet in Britain, desperately trying to stay put.

**Juvenile** – Someone who looks much younger than they really are. If attractive with it, can be used for sexual entrapment and later blackmail.

**Level** – Degree of security clearance.

**Meet** – *A* meet is usually clandestine or about a clandestine operation. *To* meet is going off to the pub with the chaps.

**Network** – Organisation of cells or individuals all providing information, and all complaining about their expenses.

**Neutralise** – Take care of any particular threat in a reasonably civilised manner, e.g. if someone has been shot, at least it was quick and he didn't feel it.

**Offed** – Someone who has been neutralised.

**PF** – Personal File. What everyone wants to see, but never does.

**Recruit** – To get someone to work for you. Even if he or she thinks he's working for someone else.

**Relay** – Simple technique (closing/opening window, etc.) to convey basic information (yes/no, safe/unsafe, it's cold/hot in here).

**Safe house** – Somewhere totally unconnected with your intelligence organisation where you can meet agents, sources, etc. in perfect safety. Or so you think.

**Screen** – Act of evaluating an individual or the information they possess to see if either can be trusted. The more someone or something is screened, the more doubtful they become.

**Sleeper** – Agent or source left well alone (and under deep cover) until needed for something important.

**Source** – Someone or something that wittingly or unwittingly gives you information you may or may not be able to use. But which is useful in making out expense claims.

**Spoilt goods** – a) A defector who may well be a double agent; b) Information that already is out of date.

**Swallow** – (Translated from the Russian) A female agent who seduces a prospective male source.

**Take-out** – The act of cutting short an operation the other side has mounted, often without so much as an 'excuse me' or 'by your leave'.

**Under cover** – A direct employee of an intelligence organisation pretending to be something else. And not always very successfully.

**Wet job** – (Translated from the Russian) A job that may well end in raised voices, even violence.

**Zap** – How cowboys talk about wet jobs.

# THE AUTHOR

Phil Kimby would like it known that he has never worked for SIS, MI5, the CIA, KGB or Sushi Incorporated. Nor does he know where these organisations are located, or who runs them. So would they please take the taps off his phone, and stop following him in the street.

He lives variously in South London, Sydney, Sao Paulo and St. Gallen, Switzerland, accompanied by a particularly vicious breed of bull terrier.

Editor's Note: Following the receipt of this unsolicited manuscript someone telephoned to say that there was not a word of truth in any of it. However contact with this person was mysteriously broken at about the time he or she developed hysterics. The exact last words were "Come on guys, I only meant it as a joke . . . I'm not really still annoyed about Vienna . . . honestly . . ."

# THE BLUFFER'S GUIDES

Planned or in preparation:

Abroad
Architecture
Banking
Beliefs
The Classics
Contemporary Cinema
Defence
Finance
Foreign Affairs
Gambling
Law
Modern Art
Opera
Poker
Politics
Psychology
Public Relations
Rugby
Secretaries
Selling
Ski-ing

The USA
The Australians
The British
The French
The Germans
The Spanish

Amsterdam
Berlin
Hong Kong
London
Moscow
New York